Bluebird Songs
Volume I

By: Edward Kenny

Bluebird Publishing—Lindenhurst, NY
ISBN: 978-0578-50111-6
Library of Congress Control Number: 2019905818
Bluebird Songs | Edward Kenny
Available formats: eBook | paperback distribution

Contact: bluebirdsongspub@gmail.com

Acknowledgements

Dedicated to my wife, children, parents, brothers and friends. Their love is my greatest success.

With the deepest gratitude to the talented music composers with whom I have collaborated. Special thanks to my songwriting partner Val Angrosini for his brilliant compositions, voice, musicianship and friendship.

Forward

Bluebird Songs is a sampling of lyrics and poems written by Edward Kenny. Although Ed has written many songs with several composers, the lyrics contained in this collection have not yet been set to music. The book categorizes the works into affairs of the heart, the mind, the spirit, the soul, history and society.

Table of Contents

Affairs of the Heart 1
Among the Clouds 2
Beautiful Again 4
Better Half 5
Center of My Universe 8
Danger of a Kiss 9
Emerald Mirage 11
Flowerman 12
Forbidden City 14
Forgiving 16
Future, Present, Past 18
Gentle Hands 20
A Glimpse of Paradise 22
Golden Strawberries 23
Leonides of the Mediterranean Sea 25
Mary Star of the Sea 27
Natural Beauty 31
A Night 33
On the Beach Alone 35
Once 36
One Kiss 37
Outside And Within 39
Quietly 40
Secrets of the Sand 42
Sunrise on the Sea 44
To the Love of My Life 45
Valerie 46

A Woman like You...48

The Mind *51*
Alien on Montague Street 52
Beach 34ᵗʰ Street...54
The Burning Sailor 57
Castle of Conch Shell...59
The Chameleon..61
Ever Wonder..63
If I Could Talk to Johnny 65
It's Up to You...67
The Japanese Flowering Cherry......................................69
The Kid 72
The Mud Flap Girl 74
Painting by Numbers 76
Private Eye 78
The Sea Witch 80
The Tune Suffering 82
View from an Expressway Overpass 84
Woman of the Id..85

The Spirit 87
Believe...88
Bet You Always Knew..90
A Better Half 92
Butterfly..93
Emerald Green..94
The Light 96
Today's The Day 97

The Soul 99
Checkmate..100

The Joke 102

<u>History</u> 104
Bill Of Rights 105

<u>Society</u> 108
Another Angel Flies 109
Australia 111
Balderdash 113
Desalegn 116
Indian Summer 119
Invincible 120
Roberto 122
Shadow of the Cheetah 124
Sights of a Rifle 126
Spirit in the Air 128
Tales of the Forgotten Sea 130
Tiny Soldiers 131
Tragic Flaw 133
About the Author 137

Affairs of the Heart...

Among the Clouds

The countless stars up in the skies,
I'd trade them all to see your eyes,
To be there when they glisten with a smile,
And up here in this windy perch
I see the world just out of reach,
It will be ours in a little while.

The silver lining up above
That holds the form and shape of love,
It wonders why we never hear its call.
Our dreams are tiny fire lights
That flicker through the endless nights,
They've traveled far although they may be small.

And we're walking here among the clouds,
We're so close and so far away,
And the shadows are upon us now,
But someday they will blow away.
And we're walking here among the clouds,
We're on the border of the day,
Soon we'll peer beyond these misty shrouds
And see the colors light our way.

The rain is falling on your face,
My love don't cry there is a place
Where one day all our troubles will be gone.
So, strip the bonds of weeks and years,
And touch the dew of happy tears,
And wait with me to hear the sounds of dawn.

And we're walking here among the clouds,
We're so close and so far away,
And the shadows are upon us now,
But someday they will blow away.
And we're walking here among the clouds,
We're on the border of the day,
Soon we'll peer beyond these misty shrouds
And see the colors light our way.

Beautiful Again

Did you think the ship would wander?
When the night came, go astray?
Did you think that it would falter?
In the darkness lose its way?

Our love is a lighthouse shining,
Guiding us through any storm,
It has been our silver lining,
It has kept us safe and warm.

And as I look at the horizon,
Of where we're going, where we've been,
In every sunrise, every sunset,
You are beautiful again.

You fear the coming winter?
The wave weathering the rock?
Well, in the land of forever
There's no ticking of the clock.

On a voyage we are sailing
To the island of our dreams,
Our love conquers any failing,
Heaven's closer than it seems.

And as I look at the horizon,
Of where we're going, where we've been,
In every sunrise, every sunset,
You are beautiful again.

Better Half

All the people that wander the city
At a speed that's out of control
They're the chaotic body politic,
It's a body without a soul.

And they're crashing into each other,
Like waves into a ship at sea,
But still that small but intrepid vessel,
It is carrying you and me.

And they don't see what is a mystery,
All because they haven't a clue,
Yet they stand on top of their soap boxes,
Tell us what it is we should do.

And it's a small percentage of voices
Drowning truth that cannot be heard,
It's a blessing that you are my solace
Because the world is so absurd.

I place my face against your face
And we caress and hold on tight,
Off we go to our secret place
Where the stars dress the dark of night.

And soon will reverie replace
All the sadness and all the blight,
Where we are hidden from the chase
'Til the madness of the first light.

The luck was all mine
On the day that I met you
And if you were gone,
I never could forget you.
And through all the tears,
Yes, I still would have to laugh,
Once I was complete
And you were my better half.

In a time once long ago,
We saw fire fall from the sky,
And we came close and felt it glow,
Rising higher, the flames would fly.

Year by year, we did not let go,
It inspired all we would try,
Like an eternal volcano,
Not to tire and not to die.

The luck was all mine
On the day that I met you
And if you were gone,
I never could forget you.
And through all the tears,
Yes, I still would have to laugh,
Once I was complete
And you were my better half.

All the people that wander the city
At a speed that's out of control,
They're the chaotic body politic,
It's a body without a soul.

And they're crashing into each other,
Like waves into a ship at sea,
But still that small but intrepid vessel,
It is carrying you and me.

And they don't see what is a mystery,
All because they haven't a clue,
Yet they stand on top of their soap boxes,
Tell us what it is we should do.

And it's a small percentage of voices
Drowning truth that cannot be heard,
It's a blessing that you are my solace
Because the world is so absurd.

Center of My Universe

Just like a solitary planet
Lost in an orbit all its own,
I wasn't one for feeling lonely,
Even when I was all alone.

Just like a sun that wasn't shining,
I was content with endless night,
But since the moment I first saw you,
I've seen a galaxy of light.

And what would I be without you?
Well things would just go from bad to worse,
Now all of my life is about you,
You're the center of my universe.

Just like a million men before me,
Searching the sky to find a star,
Until the first time that you touched me,
No man had ever flown so far.

Just like a star taken for granted,
Maybe you think that I don't see,
I've seen a little glimpse of heaven,
And you mean the world to me.

And what would I be without you?
Well things would just go from bad to worse,
Now all of my life is about you,
You're the center of my universe.

Danger of A Kiss

A suggestion from the night,
As it whispers in our ears,
Is it the doorway to delight?
Or the first drop of our tears?

Like the tide, a mood can shift,
And we're untethered from the moor,
A little closer do we drift,
A little further from the shore.

Such is the danger of a kiss
And the passion we pursue,
But I'd jump into the abyss
Just to fall in love with you.

In the calm before the storm
The dry earth will crave the rain,
And the clouds above will form
To bring the pleasure and pain.

But if someone knows my name
And each hair upon my head,
There's a reason why you came
To my life and to my bed.

Such is the danger of a kiss
And the passion we pursue,
But I'd jump into the abyss
Just to fall in love with you.

I've heard waves come crashing down
In a tiny ocean shell,
And I was drawn to your town,
By the tolling of a bell.

Was it only happenstance?
Or was it our destiny?
To kiss, it was worth the chance,
To live so dangerously.

Such is the danger of a kiss
And the passion we pursue,
But I'd jump into the abyss
Just to fall in love with you.

Emerald Mirage

The foggy night has made it clearer,
The image that I sometimes see,
A girl that moves closer and closer,
Just as she fades away from me.

And so, questions carve my expressions,
Beyond beauty, what can be learned?
The fog glows for her emerald eyes,
But is my gaze at her returned?

With tips that sting and soothe the arrows fly
In an emotional barrage,
There's more to this vision than meets the eye,
Beyond this emerald mirage.

Am I beguiled by desert magic?
This apparition seems surreal,
Even though I hold her in my arms,
Still I must wonder if she is real.

With icy heat the wind will whisper,
In confusion my eyes are marred,
I know I've been touched by this lover
In places that are healed and scarred.

With tips that sting and soothe the arrows fly
In an emotional barrage,
There's more to this vision than meets the eye,
Beyond this emerald mirage.

Flowerman

Touched the hand of flowerman,
Magic was, magic is again,
Because magic is reached when,
You reach out as far as you can,
And touch roots that stand to bend,
Well I feel my roots deeper than,
The deepest ocean sand,
The deepest ocean's sand.

Touched the hand of flowerman,
Touched my eyes, and the aura shows,
Harvest is for those who sow,
And if the sun fell far below,
Blades of grass lost their sharp glow,
There would still be a green shadow.
He'd find a way to grow,
He'd find a way to grow.

Flowerman in truth,
I am much like you,
Garden for a life,
Yellows and maroons,
Flower for a wife,
Mellow afternoons,
Dreams of dahlias,
That touch the moon.

Touched the hand of flowerman,
Watering tiny, tiny, seeds,

Is all I will ever need,
For on sweet whispers flowers breathe,
And they breathe back memories,
Of the heart of the soil still in me,
Flowerman will always be,
Flowerman will always be.

Forbidden City

Tonight, I crossed the deepest river,
With a single step I took,
I learned what no one ever taught me,
And it only took one look.

It was just the length of an eyelash,
All it took to pass that space,
When I could start to feel the fire,
We were standing face to face.

And oh, that girl was pretty...
I met her in the glow,
Of the Forbidden City,
Where few men ever go.

A moment changed my life forever,
As I wrapped my arms around
The woman there beneath the surface,
So beautifully profound.

A boy is like a lost explorer,
Who emerges as a man,
Who passes the point of no return
And cannot go back again.

And oh, that girl was pretty...
I met her in the glow,
Of the Forbidden City,
Where few men ever go.

If she never whispered softly,
If I never knew her name,
Just the glimmer of her smiling,
And I'd never be the same.

And oh that girl was pretty...
I met her in the glow,
Of the Forbidden City,
Where few men ever go.

Forgiving

The strongest hands can tremble,
Thoughts will disassemble,
A golden throat will quiver,
Struggling to deliver

The words that I've been thinking,
It's me who sent you sinking,
You really should be sailing,
My fault and my failing.

Forgiving me, forgiving you,
Whatever was the issue,
I only want to kiss you,
Forgiving me, forgiving you,
Whatever are the problems,
Somehow, we always solve them.

The fleetest foot will stumble,
Truth has made me humble,
The tightest lips can open,
Say what should be spoken.

The gift I should have taken,
The love that was forsaken,
No longer will I squander,
Angel from up yonder.

Forgiving me, forgiving you,
Whatever was the issue,
I only want to kiss you,

Forgiving me, forgiving you,
Whatever are the problems,
Somehow, we always solve them.

Future, Present, Past

I watch you when you're sleeping,
When you're totally unaware,
I close my eyes and swallow,
And I stifle a little tear.

I watch you from a distance,
When you don't even know I'm there,
I know what I've been given,
And I whisper a silent prayer.

Once upon a time a star was shining,
In the darkness of the sky,
But before I came upon it shining,
Long ago it had to die.
And it makes me think about forever,
And how long a love can last,
But I will still love you that much longer,
In the future, present, past.

I hold you while you're weeping,
Sometimes the one who made you sad,
I listen to you laughing,
And telling me my jokes are bad.

I believe I will love you,
And always your love will return,
A shining thing enduring,
When the stars no longer burn.

Once upon a time a star was shining,
In the darkness of the sky,
But before I came upon it shining,
Long ago it had to die.
And it makes me think about forever,
And how long a love can last,
But I will still love you that much longer,
In the future, present, past

Gentle Hands

I'm not the guy on the cover
Of those romance books,
I don't make a lot of money,
Like white collar crooks,

But still I know that I love you,
My feelings are real.
And all I have is a lifetime
To make sure you'll feel...

Gentle hands in the morning,
Just as I walk away,
And a kiss in the evening,
To say how was your day,
And a word of compassion,
When things go terribly wrong,
Gentle hands you'll be finding
Are remarkably strong.

You're a girl who deserves better,
Wish I could give more,
But I have demons to conquer,
That old human flaw.

Still I believe if I'm trying,
Improving each day,
We can put our hands together,
And we'll find our way.

Gentle hands in the morning,
Just as I walk away,
And a kiss in the evening,
To say how was your day,
And a word of compassion,
When things go terribly wrong,
Gentle hands you'll be finding
Are remarkably strong.

Fact can be stranger
Than the fiction they say,
Fact is I love you
In a storybook way.

Gentle hands in the nighttime,
When you will be caressed,
And the light of a new day
On a life that is blessed,
And a heart full of passion,
Someone forever to hold,
Gentle hands you'll be finding,
They will never get old.

A Glimpse of Paradise

In but a few days I found myself again.
Once I was lost...
Lost in my worries, my work, myself.
Maybe I'd forgotten who I really am,
And what you really mean to me.
And then I caught a glimpse of paradise!
Oh, not in the twinkling diamonds in the deep night skies,
Or in the sparkling silver sands,
Or even in the turquoise mystery of the sea...
Not in the golden sunrise,
Or in the soothing palm trees,
Or even in the many colors of a magical rainbow...
For I caught a glimpse of paradise in you.
I saw it in your smile, your eyes, the child in you,
And the wisdom...
I saw your sensuality, rising from the ocean,
Shimmering as you approached me on the beach,
Looking like a vision.
Now I know how much I needed a moment in my life
That will never end...
And a place that I can steal away to again and again,
To look at the one I love,
And to rediscover my soul mate.
Now that I have that moment,
I will cherish it in my memory like an enchanted island,
Bordered by a heavenly horizon.
And I know that I will always see a glimpse of paradise in
you.

Golden Strawberries

Sunlight teases my eyelids,
Morning breathes into me,
Seems like a nice day outside,
I'm not getting up to see

I want so much to kiss you,
But I see you're still asleep,
Your gentle arms, a ribbon,
Wrap the tiny gift of me.

Golden clouds surround your face,
They're so fragrant in the breeze,
Like an echo of your name,
The scent: golden strawberries.

Highlights in the summer,
Reeds in autumn wind,
Children in a wheat field,
Running hand in hand.

And then as I grasp for something,
And my sleepy voice requests
Golden wings to carry me
And then gently let me rest.

Sorry, but you startled me,
While I took my turn to dream,
Then awake it's good to see,
Still we linger in the gleam...

Of the golden strawberries,
That cascade from up above,
And, oh what a day this will be,
With the princess of my love.

Highlights in the summer,
Reeds in autumn wind,
Children in a wheat field,
Running hand in hand.

Leonides of the Mediterranean Sea

A moment to awaken,
Came many years ago,
Before his book was written,
Before his lamp would glow.

It was a time for dreaming,
A respite from the race,
For what his eyes were seeing,
Brought a smile to his face.

And it was a star he called Abraham,
Bright in the sky of what was to be.
This was the vision of Leonides,
Leonides, of the Mediterranean Sea.

The night before tomorrow,
When evil would not fail,
Brought suffering and sorrow,
But courage would prevail.

In time the tide was conquered,
With hatred in its den,
A dream could be realized,
A child would live again.

And it was a star he called Abraham,
Bright in the sky of what was to be.
This was the vision of Leonides,
Leonides, of the Mediterranean Sea.

A holocaust survivor,
In World War II, in Greece,
Had to be a warrior,
To have a son in peace.

A partisan, a hero,
Believer `til the end,
Who brought to America,
Someone I call my friend

And it was a star he called Abraham,
Bright in the sky of what was to be.
This was the vision of Leonides,
Leonides, of the Mediterranean Sea.

Mary Star of the Sea

The color came back to the face,
Of the girl on the pillow case,
It's funny how she sensed the gloom…
The quiet of a crowded room.

She sat up to see mother's chair,
Neither she, nor her sisters there,
Pneumonia in a single blow…
At four years old she had to go…

Off with strangers to foster care,
Where she would stay a second year,
Until her father came to say,
Mary, we're going home today.

And she's telling the story
Over a cup of tea,
In her beauty and glory,
Mary star of the sea.
And she says work and worry,
Brought her longevity,
In her beauty and glory,
Mary star of the sea.

Her father started a new life,
With a stepmother as a wife,
Earned his way by the bricks he'd lay,
Leaving Mary back home to stay…

With a woman that goodness fails,
Striking with a cat 'o nine tails,
And when daddy saw her black eye,
His daughter felt she had to lie.

Down and away her eyes they dove,
Daddy I fell against the stove,
Off to bed, 'til another day,
When she would work and never play.

And she's telling the story
Over a cup of tea,
In her beauty and glory,
Mary star of the sea.
And she says work and worry,
Brought her longevity,
In her beauty and glory,
Mary star of the sea.

She served the old witch faithfully,
Until at nineteen she was free,
When her stepmother's life was done,
Mary's had really just begun.

They called her "step-ins," fast she dressed,
And all the boys were so impressed,
From the Empire State Building
She saw what hopes and dreams could bring.

Then came the pain she'd felt before,
The loss of loved ones to the war,
Not by bullets or shrapnel parts,
But by sights that wound minds and hearts.

And she's telling the story
Over a cup of tea,
In her beauty and glory,
Mary star of the sea.
And she says work and worry,
Brought her longevity,
In her beauty and glory,
Mary star of the sea.

One brother came from Anzio,
A silver star's baggage in tow,
From New Guinea another too,
A bronze star, but, not who they knew.

One in the navy stayed in the states,
Lost to lung cancer of all fates,
And one who did not even enlist,
Landed on the K.I.A. List.

One brother's babies whisked away,
And yet through it all she would stay
With a smile by her father's side,
Caring for him 'til he died.

And she's telling the story
Over a cup of tea,
In her beauty and glory,
Mary star of the sea.
And she says work and worry,
Brought her longevity,
In her beauty and glory,
Mary star of the sea.

Then she married the love of her life,
He her husband, she his wife,
They raised three sons in a house of wood,
Made a better neighborhood.

And when a stroke made her man so sick,
Her actions were heroic,
And she hid the pain she felt inside,
With the private tears she cried.

Now she'll give you a smile or song,
Don't argue, 'cause you'll be wrong,
And she'll make you laugh with a jest,
For a century the world's been blessed.

And she's telling the story
Over a cup of tea,
In her beauty and glory,
Mary star of the sea.
And she says work and worry,
Brought her longevity,
In her beauty and glory,
Mary star of the sea.

Natural Beauty

They're stunning and they're striking,
God, she's got beautiful eyes,
I notice they're brightening
At me, and not other guys.

She's not polished and painted
To make her shiny and new,
And inside she's not tainted,
Her goodness comes shining through.

And maybe it's shallow,
I'm just a fellow
Who's in love.
I just see what I see,
And she came to me
From above.

And she's a natural beauty,
Rising above the rest,
And I'm just doing my duty,
Telling you I've been blessed.

Her celestial body,
I can feel in her embrace,
With her arms all around me,
I can float in outer space.

But the sad thing that remains,
We're here just a little while,

And still, through anything that pains,
I will always have her smile.

And maybe it's shallow,
I'm just a fellow
Who's in love.
I just see what I see,
And she came to me
From above.

And she's a natural beauty,
Rising above the rest,
And I'm just doing my duty,
Telling you I've been blessed.

A Night

Like mood movie music, last night, she told him to stay,
And they rolled together like waves on a beach of play,
Holding each other in the peace of the night,
Letting a ring around the moon reflect their future bright.

And they talked of their past dreary and sweet,
Of the long search for this moment engraved in sore feet.
And the earth wrapped them like butterflies in a cocoon,
As the winds of the coming storm set its sights on their ruin.

But at least they had a night,
And their love was their last sight,
And the world could end tomorrow,
And they know through all the sorrow,
That at least they had a night.

A siren appeared cameo in his sleepy dream,
He was soon to be an actor cast into the wrong scene.
A hammer of daylight shattered his eyes,
While the sounds of death's voice droned in the skies.

He ran to the window to jump to his senses,
But the world screamed below dying defenseless.
He turned to the bed to see if last night was a dream,
In it slept his new lover, surreal in this odd scene.

But at least they had a night,
And their love was their last sight,
And the world could end tomorrow,
And they know through all the sorrow,
That at least they had a night.

Panic's voice sent his feet running helter-skelter,
He ran to wake her and take her to shelter,
But he felt the oven hot walls as he tripped on the window drape,
He realized that the world was in flame with no escape.

He shed a tear whispering love vows in spades,
Alone in fear he knew some folks can sleep through air raids,
And as the building collapsed to the pavement below,
He held her in the only dream she'd ever know.

But at least they had a night,
And their love was their last sight,
And the world could end tomorrow,
And they know through all the sorrow,
That at least they had a night.

On the Beach Alone

The sounds of the day
Trickled down through the caves
To the spaces the rocks left vacant.
And her hand in my hand,
Her footsteps next to mine in the sand, were noticeably absent.
And I felt I could pawn
This man she's adored
And he wouldn't bring a cent.
For her hand in my hand,
Her footsteps next to mine in the sand,
Were noticeably absent.
She wore two bathing suits,
One red, and one blue,
And they lasted spring to fall,
But she is many colors, like a peacock...
And now the sky's not grey,
Nor is the bay,
For today there is no color at all.
For her hand in my hand,
Her footsteps next to mine in the sand...

Once

Once in a lifetime comes a day like this,
All in an instant of a magic kiss,
Then does a prince become a king,
Just as the princess is a queen,
And at last paradise is seen...

Once there is courage and a chance to take,
Then from a slumber does the sleeper wake,
That was the day I took your hand,
We built a mountain out of sand,
And we knew forever we could stand...

Once we could leave the earth and learn to fly,
Then nothing could bring us down from the sky,
Dancing on air away we glide,
Home is the place called "side by side,"
And love will never be denied...

Once you were there I was forever changed,
It was as if the planets rearranged,
And from the moment that we met,
Everything else I could forget,
Never again feel a regret...
Once.

One Kiss

Some people have to laugh at us,
Empty barrels making noise,
They're experts on the birds and bees,
But not on the girls and boys.

And when our perfect moment comes,
They will say that it won't last,
But love lives in the present and
The future and the past.

Life has always been in color,
But the world sees black and white,
Every piece would fit like clockwork,
If we'd only get it right.

And as I stood at the crossroads
Of desolation and bliss,
I knew I was blessed to find you,
And I knew it with one kiss.

With their heads full of equations,
They will calculate and plot,
They'll draw lines to infinity,
Not connect a single dot.

They'll wonder what our secret is,
As if we could just recite
How to create a miracle
From the void of endless night.

Life has always has been in color,
But the world sees black and white,
Every piece would fit like clockwork,
If we'd only get it right.

And as I stood at the crossroads
Of desolation and bliss,
I knew I was blessed to find you,
And I knew it with one kiss.

Outside And Within

When a woman of beauty
Had captured my eye,
I found physical beauty
Was often a lie.

When a woman of substance
Would turn on my mind,
I found people of brilliance
Are sometimes so blind.

But for all of my doubting,
I won't doubt again,
You're a beautiful woman,
Outside and within.

When a woman of honor
Had said she'd be true,
I found words have no honor,
But actions still do.

When a woman so loving
Would plan with her heart,
I found people stop loving
When plans fall apart.

But for all of my doubting,
I won't doubt again,
You're a beautiful woman,
Outside and within.

Quietly

They tell me I should stop believing,
That I'm the one I've been deceiving,
To lock my dreams up on a shelf,
That there is no jolly old elf.

Saint Valentine and the Easter Bunny
Are just two guys out to make money,
And the world isn't turned by love,
Or in the hands of God above.

Holed up here on a mountain peak,
I am the fugitive they seek,
Their dogs can bark, spotlights can glow,
Say what they want, I still won't go...
Quietly into the night,
No, I won't give in without a fight.
Quietly into the sun,
Live as an outlaw, then die as one.

You say the bloom is off the roses,
Your door was open, now it closes,
We were lovers, but now we're friends,
That's just the way the story ends.

The magic shamrock's just a clover,
The fairytale we lived is over,
But, still the music plays in me,
Even if it plays quietly.

Holed in here on a mountain peak,
I am the fugitive they seek,
Their guns can shoot, bullhorns can blow,
Say what they want, I still won't go...
Quietly into the night,
No, I won't give in without a fight.
Quietly into the sun, live as an outlaw, then die as one.

Secrets of the Sands

An artist paints a picture,
That soon will fade from reach,
A pallet full of secrets
Left hidden on the beach…

Of circles bound together,
Boundary lines for games,
Words of love in valentines
In which we wrote our names.

I see us there together,
With feelings in our hands,
Before erased forever
Would be our secrets of the sands.

The grains slipped through our fingers,
Pink sunsets kissed the day,
The tide rolled all around us
And washed our words away.

Ghosts return for mementos,
And sing in empty shells,
The echoes of the stories
The sand no longer tells.

I see us there together,
With feelings in our hands,
Before erased forever
Would be our secrets of the sands.

Alone I still draw pictures,
If you come to the shores,
You'll my name there longing
To lie again with yours.

I see us there together,
With feelings in our hands,
Before erased forever
Would be our secrets of the sands.

Sunrise on the Sea

If endings must be tragic,
Beginnings doomed to fail,
If clouds dot the horizon
As every ship sets sail,

If dreams are meant to vanish,
And colors drawn to fade,
If there's a broken promise
For everyone that's made,

If birds that we see flying
Will disappear from view,
If nothing is forever,
If true love isn't true...

Then why does our love grow warmer,
And shine so brilliantly?
Is it something like the sunrise
Each morning on the sea?

On the sea,
On the sea,
Our love is like the sunrise
On the sea.

To the Love of My Life

Recently, a friend of mine lost his wife.
This struck me with a different kind of pain
Than I'd ever felt before.
Although I'd lost some of those who were closest to me,
This was somehow a side of midnight I'd never seen.
I put myself into my friend's position
And tried to imagine a morning without you,
But it wasn't very long before
I discarded this attempt at empathy.
I dropped it from my hands like a live wire.
I jumped away, startled, shocked,
Vowing never to dare test this electric adversary again.
And so, it seems I cannot bear to think
Of how cold my bed would be without you…
Even on a summer night,
Or how many times I'd find a situation
Where we would have laughed together,
And now I would cry,
Or how sad a person can be,
Or how lonesome and full of despair.
I can only think of how very much I love you…
I can only see you in my dreams,
Touch you in my waking moments,
Marvel at how happy you have made me.
I can only think of being with you forever,
Because life without you would be to me no life at all.

Valerie

The setting sun took flight,
Into the winds of endless night,
To spread warmth between our eyes,
Like two stars dancing in the skies.
A vision came in sight,
Two candles were alight.
In such eerie blind times,
When poets are lost in between the lines,
Of what their spirits should be,
And all that their wide eyes don't see.
And so, before we could ever know,
Rivers of love lives would flow.
Through forest green hills with you,
On winding dusty highways of truth,
We sung as romance played its tune,
But Valerie there was more than us two.
And before the dawn was blue,
Passionate meteors flew.
And a festival of life filled the night,
A solar sight of the candle-mime,
Flickering the figures of our futures on the wall,
Oh, we lit summer onto fall,
With more than flames wrapped within your purple shawl,
More than all of the sweet names we called,
We have love together, but that's not all.
The dawn was blue,
Two green leaves of the morning,
Landed on a stream of spring,
Valerie and me so close,

But not everything,
For bells ring only when men pull a string.
Lord give us the music to bring,
You, to the love songs we so freely sing.
Oh, Valerie come climbing with me,
To find peaks of love in all that we seek,
Valerie, I'm a gypsy in your arms,
To wander forever in your charms,
But as we sleep the nebulae storms
Where will we wake when the wild ocean calms?
Our love and our lives will be gone,
If not, our souls still carry on.

A Woman like You

It doesn't happen often,
Sightings have been rare,
Know to cause a double take,
Elicit a stare.

The green flash at the sunset,
Comets in the blue,
The shot you never hear,
The one that hits you.

Then all at once I saw her
And she struck me blind,
And so was joined the battle,
Between heart and mind.

All the crazy things we say,
Foolish things we do,
Just happens when men meet
A woman like you.

And gods might have their goddesses,
And kings their consorts too,
But I have something they don't have,
It's a woman like you.

When fact collides with fiction,
Dreaming while awake,
A heart feeling so full,
It's about to break.

Through time and space, I'm speeding,
Fighting for control,
And breaking into pieces,
While becoming whole.

One minute I'll be laughing,
Then I want to cry,
Never felt so much alive,
Love's the reason why.

I'm sad for what I'm losing,
Glad for what is new,
It's all worth it for
A woman like you.

And gods might have their goddesses
And kings their consorts too,
But I have something they don't have,
It's a woman like you.

The Mind…

Alien on Montague Street

I walked the street for all to see,
On a bright November day,
When I came to visit Brooklyn
From some billion miles away.

And the street sign said Montague,
And I wondered who he was.
Was he dead like the animals
Who filled store windows with furs?

I thought about the history,
And the wives' tales that I'd heard,
But no one said a word to me,
Even tirdy tird an' tird.

The vehicles were primitive,
The drivers, Neanderthal,
And the street was held in its place
By brown stones that formed a wall.

But of all the eyes that spied me,
Not a single one was fazed,
Although I'm green and circular,
Not a single brow was raised.

The fastest thing I'd ever seen
Was running off with a purse,
While a fallen old matriarch
Lay there shouting out a curse.
Then a brown horse and a blue man

Hit the asphalt trail in chase,
The crowd filed into O.T.B.,
I guess to bet on the race.

But of all the eyes that spied me,
Not a single one was fazed,
Although I'm green and circular,
Not a single brow was raised.

The street ended at a railing,
And below me were the piers,
And there upon a wooden bench
Lay a beard grown long with years.

I said, "Are you Rip Van Winkle?"
But the dirty man seemed deaf,
He just pointed to Manhattan,
Took my satellite and left.

And so, there I was left stranded,
By the city by the sea,
When I came upon a lady,
She was just as green as me.

And I could see she held a torch,
So, I climbed through her inside,
Signaled to the passing planes,
But just couldn't hitch a ride.

But of all the eyes that spied me,
Not a single one was fazed,
Although I'm green and circular,
Not a single brow was raised.

Beach 34th Street

Potholes show their teeth to the car,
You hit Queens, you know where you are.
I'm taking the curves on raw nerve,
Counting on luck I don't deserve,
Headed just south of the great beyond,
Now that the shocks in my heart are gone.
Dancing alone with empty arms,
Holding on to what is all gone,
Having loved and lost from afar,
I'm too young to cry in a bar,
So, tonight I'll just have a beer,
And shed a tear under the stars.

The hitchhiker's wiggling her jeans,
Not that I don't know what that means,
But I'm keeping a dream in reach,
I see it alone on the beach,
But then just as I pass her to get there,
I'm left as puzzled as her stare,
'Though the car windows are open,
The body's not fully broke in,
And the face is in sweaty beads,
And the wind scatters them like seeds,
And they fly off into the weeds
And lie there where loneliness bleeds.

The bungalows go down like drugs,
This is a good place to get mugged,
Far Rockaway is a ghost town

A resort town burned to the ground,
And now the A-Train cracks on the tracks,
Like the bones in a broken back.
It's September, the beach empty,
Someone saw me they'd say "crazy,"
Because I'm out past the jetty,
Out where I know no one can save me,
But I will still swim back in time,
After I find my own beauty.

When the boardwalk stands have all burned,
You know the season has badly turned,
But from their scars so much they're learned,
Lost some things honestly earned.
Well, I've burned myself down like them,
But I will build it up again,
And I will collect my thoughts,
And just as I do in sports,
On the fields and stickball courts,
Running wild in cut-off shorts,
Once again, I will win.

Away like a bare backed Tarzan,
Out here where no one can see me
The waves try, but they don't scare me,
They fill up the grey rocks inside me,
Like clues to a mystery.
Now I'm so glad to be out of school,
Not to have to prove that I'm cool,
I can live by a new set of rules,
I can start using all of my tools.
I'm the stranger that few ever knew,
But I found peace in the green and blue,

And I suddenly know what to do,
My dream girl, today I'll meet you.

The Burning Sailor

The sailor saw the fire
Illuminate the mast,
And he would look no higher,
The clouds they seemed so vast.

But would St. Elmo help him
Beyond this raging sea?
He felt the storm inside him
Burn electricity.

A mistress of Barbary
Was comforting and warm,
But with little jewelry
He couldn't keep her long.

Her beauty was transmuted
By simple alchemy.
His roaring voice was muted
By mere hostility.

When an anger so repressed
Is brushed back like a mane,
Then its body is redressed,
Its volume rearranged.
And for the burning sailor
It surfaces again.

The moon is not a pirate
Who steals away the night,

While one shore may imply it,
Another one will rise,

Yet through the orange billows,
Beneath the ink of rain,
The sailor cries, "St. Elmo,
The sea has turned to flame!"

When an anger so repressed
Is brushed back like a mane,
Then its body is redressed,
Its volume rearranged.
And for the burning sailor
It surfaces again.

Castle of Conch Shell

His head falls in reckless flight,
The sandman's sleep wakes the night,
Seemingly forsaken plight.
Acrobat's mistaken flight
When death is robbed of seconds.
The knitted web holds him tight,
In the dark his eyes snow-blind,
In the hearth of cabin kind,
An ultraviolet light shines,
Lays a path above the pines.
As a blizzard of feathers
Is vacuumed to take-off lights,
Knitting a rainbow of snow,
The night colors show their glow,
Birds are reborn from the floor,
And through the door
More and more, score by score,
A million strong.
Off to the cliff of slaughter,
Diver reflected in water,
Shallow depth is life's border,
A brain chime gives the order,
Fly again forgotten prayer,
Rock melts like molten mortar.
Outside the tension fuse blows,
Waves calm and sow the hole closed,
Outside the flow no one knows,
A tiny craft he rows and rows.
Molecules dance in cycle,
A drop in the sun he glows.

But the past is foreign calm.
He breaks the surface beyond,
'Till the seven seas are gone,
Only the eighth lies beyond,
His fins are free, gills can breathe,
His wonderment does believe,
Endless tricks lie up his sleeve.
The siren's song makes him long,
Sun in his lungs makes him strong,
And he flies high and dives low,
Direction's course is the wuerth.
"Higher, higher" the cry,
"Call me again to die."
Wake more and more alive.
Sweet sword, scatter this cloud,
Sweet song sound, sing aloud,
Claw above pain and blood,
Swim to touch whitened mud,
Fly above purple plains,
Sky lit by turquoise rains.
Alas! Lies the castle.
Familiar and strange, so sanely insane,
So peaceful and plain.
Mermaids coyly call,
Upon water walls,
Combat with the tusks,
Riding on mollusks.
Treasure within inches,
Cut the last pinchers.
He claims his new realm,
Ring the kingdom bell,
(crowned) Subjects all marked him well,
'Till someone stepped on this tiny, tiny conch shell.

The Chameleon

I'm not the man I used to be,
And yet they still are hunting me,
A wanted poster's not a face,
A shadow from another place.

And if you think that you knew me,
People see what they want to see,
Whatever colors pleased their eyes
Were my defense and my disguise.

I threw a bottle from the beach,
Where dreams are here, and then they are gone,
My words are floating out of reach,
But once I was the chameleon.

I left you with some mythic tales,
A train that echoes down the rails,
Out where the outlaws turn to dust,
And golden ages live to rust.

Tell the ladies they'll be missed,
Especially those I never kissed,
The ghosts that haunt the most you see,
Brought the best colors out in me.

I threw a bottle from the beach,
Where dreams are here, and then they are gone,
My words are floating out of reach,
But once I was the chameleon.

I tried my best to be so true,
But covered up when I was blue,
When I felt timid, I'd be bold,
Held out longer than most could hold.

And if you follow in my tracks,
Well, then it's time to face the facts,
Don't make a promise in the night,
You can't keep in the morning light.

I threw a bottle from the beach,
Where dreams are here, and then they are gone,
My words are floating out of reach,
But once I was the chameleon.

Ever Wonder

I still see them playing in the sunshine,
Just like two bear cubs on the run.
Boys will be boys, but in the meantime,
Then who are we to spoil their fun?

I never noticed as we lost the light,
December days leave little time,
To teach all about what is wrong and right,
Then Cinderella hears the chime.

Do you ever wonder what God is thinking?
How much it matters? Who's to blame?
They're only children, so why not let them be?
They're only playing a game.

I see someone in another instance,
We too were bear cubs on the run.
The grown-ups watched, but kept their distance,
Yet things got passed on to a son.

And I guess they'd say we turned out alright,
We learned the things we had to learn,
'Though we teach about what is wrong and right,
Do we stand up when it's our turn?

Do you ever wonder what God is thinking?
How much it matters? Who's to blame?
They're only children, so why not let them be?
They're only playing a game.

I still see them on the shoreline,
The endless ocean was so blue,
Friendship walks along such a fine line,
One day they will learn what is true.

I never noticed as the tide went out,
The grains of sand it took away.
The years pass so quickly, there is no doubt,
We can't afford to waste a day.

Do you ever wonder what God is thinking?
How much it matters who's to blame?
They're only children, so why not let them be?
'They're only playing a game.

If I Could Talk to Johnny

How fast that white impala,
With summer in my hair,
But in the rear view mirror,
The picture was so clear.

The adolescent gallows,
The adult in a hood,
Can't hold them off forever,
But I did what I could.

And if I could talk to Johnny,
He'd show me some tricks.
How to make it in the city,
A boy from the sticks.
Yeah, if I could talk to Johnny,
Not just as a fan,
And not as a celebrity,
Just us man to man.

I saw the sun was setting,
Just as I hit the beach,
Just holding on to freedom,
Just barely out of reach.

How could I win the lady,
And not destroy the fool?
How could I leave them laughing,
Still be the guy so cool?

And if I could talk to Johnny,
Thank you Mr. "C,"
If I never talked to Johnny,
He sure spoke to me.
Yeah, if I could talk to Johnny,
Not a boy, a man,
You didn't really die lonely,
Or without a plan.

It's Up to You

Go on complaining...
What good has it ever done?
Who listens anyway?
Seems you are the only one.

Your hesitation
Invites others to rush in,
You're finished from the start,
'Til at last you will begin.

The moon is waning
And the tide is drifting out,
But your dream is still new,
No, there isn't any doubt.

Bright inspiration
Is still burning in your breast,
Your talent is a light,
One whose flame should never rest.

This is the moment to make or break your life,
To walk the jagged edge balanced on the knife,
And those who love you have done all they can do,
Now all is said and done and it's up to you.

Go on explaining
All the reasons that you lose,
That was yesterday,
And tomorrow's what you choose.

All calculation
Is at risk in a romance,
The lady brings no luck unless you will take a chance.

There's nothing chaining
You to the ocean floor,
Even the smallest shell
Can duplicate its roar.

No situation
Is lost, without any hope,
Just look within yourself,
And you'll find a way to cope.

This the moment to make or break your life,
To walk the jagged edge balanced on the knife,
And those who love you have done all they can do,
Now all is said and done and it's up to you.

The future exists for those who insist
That tomorrow holds more than today,
And fate often twists and guides through the mist
Any ship that will find its own way.

This the moment to make or break your life,
To walk the jagged edge balanced on the knife,
And those who love you have done all they can do,
Now all is said and done and it's up to you.

The Japanese Flowering Cherry

The house was weather-beaten brown.
With shingles windblown on the ground.
Must have been two hundred years old,
And the story that I've been told
A team of horses moved it 'round.

And I suppose that is why some
Felt it stuck out, a sore thumb,
But all I know is that for me
It was where I wanted to be,
And where people wanted to come.

It stands there in my memory,
The kind that nature gives for free,
But power's the goal of your lust.
Money's the only god you trust,
So, this is hard for you to see.

The Japanese Flowering Cherry
Was something very special to me,
And for just a few good days of spring,
I would have sacrificed anything.
Yes, that old Japanese cherry tree,
Was something very special to me,
And for just a few good days in May...
But you took all that away.

And if you don't know, then you don't care,
For useless fruit most of the year,

But it is worth the useless fruit
That squashes underneath your boot,
When the pink and white flowers appear.

'Though the little corner house was brave,
The sky above would not behave,
It warned a storm was imminent.
As inland the seagulls were sent,
Soon there would be nothing left to save.

After days of winter made us wait,
The sad sheets of rain seemed to hate
This symbol of beauty to me,
As petals were blown out to sea.
And the shattered house just lay in state.

The Japanese Flowering Cherry
Was something very special to me,
And for just a few good days of spring,
I would have sacrificed anything.
Yes, that old Japanese cherry tree,
Was something very special to me,
And for just a few good days in May...
But you took all that away.

How often I've taken you to bed,
How we've waltzed around in my head,
How many times I have met you
Inside a club called the "Déjà Vu,"
Hearing all of the words we've ever said.

And I think I was wrong in hindsight,
Either that or I just wasn't right,

But no matter how I color
Your image seems to get duller
'Til it fades to only black and white.

You're the kind that just haggles and hacks,
Wielding your George Washington axe,
Ah but all of your honesty
Really means nothing much to me,
And nothing justifies your attacks.

The Japanese Flowering Cherry
Was something very special to me,
And for just a few good days of spring,
I would have sacrificed anything.
Yes, that old Japanese cherry tree,
Was something very special to me,
And for just a few good days in May...
But you took all that away.

The Kid

The king of a play hill,
Rainbow in my eyes,
The ride would be gallant,
And I'd win the prize.
Tall on the ball field,
Or writing for fame,
Living simple and long-haired,
When life was a game.

The kid, the kid,
Call me the kid,
'Cos I never intended to be writing this song,
'Cos I never intended to be here this long.

Ride into a sunset,
A heartbreaking scene,
Once legend, once hero,
Now, a selfish dream.
Western days grow shorter,
As I look around,
They saw me flying,
Said "gun that kid down."

The kid, the kid,
Call me the kid,
'Cos I never intended to be writing this song,
'Cos I never intended to be here this long.

Lord I'm an old ballad,

You give us our pen,
Startled wild stallions,
But, we write the end.
And my soul's a restless
Ghost rider of night.
Once freedom is tasted,
There's no morning light.

The kid, the kid,
Call me the kid,
'Cos I never intended to be writing this song,
'Cos I never intended to be here this long.

The Mud Flap Girl

I was driving down the highway,
Tired and alone,
She was suddenly before me,
Guess I should have known.

It's the things that come so easy,
Seldom can be real,
But in the heat of the moment,
That's not how you feel

It's to the graveyard, or to the races,
It's left to heaven and right to hell.
If you can't see me, then I can't see you,
But then I guess it's just as well.
Ignore the warnings and give it a whirl,
Following behind the mud flap girl

The mud flap girl, shining in silver in the sun,
You saw her first, and you are the only one.
Objects in mirrors are always closer than they seem,
And you've got to know what is real and what is a dream.

She's a physical perfection,
Icon to adore,
As he abandons his convictions,
Man wants nothing more?
'Til he wakes up with the object,
Of his broken heart,
That he touches without feeling,

That's the painful part.

It's to the graveyard, or to the races,
It's left to heaven and right to hell.
If you can't see me, then I can't see you,
But then I guess it's just as well.
Ignore the warnings and give it a whirl,
Following behind the mud flap girl

The mud flap girl, shining in silver in the sun,
You saw her first, and you are the only one.
Objects in mirrors are always closer than they seem,
And you've got to know what is real and what is a dream.

Painting by Numbers

From the time you are born
The lines have been drawn in advance,
Wriggling snakes on a page
To mark off the stage for the dance.
You pick up your stencil
Your tail prehensiled for movement,
And you swing from a tree,
Fly falling free to pavement.
Where the sky must be blue
And where it leads to is too far,
The boundary scares you so
You make darkness glow with the stars.
You grow out of the game
But life is the same in its fears,
So, you run to the door, but close it before light appears.
You're painting by numbers
Joining the hundreds in line,
The zeroes multiply
Forget how to cry in due time.
For language is not words
Only sounds you've heard them meaning,
You fall asleep at night
With only your sights for dreaming.
And wake with reverent shock pleading with clocks not
listening,
As they're calling to you
That everything's new, but ticking.
And stars mark off the spots
For plays without plots thickening,

As the earth quakes apart with its dying heart quickening.
Still remains a faint smell is it parallel or adjacent?
Are there little green men?
Why are we then complacent?
Yes, I know where I am
And show you I can on a map
In a universe lobe
Pointing to a globe fingers tap.
Call this, "Schenectady"
This is "you" and "me" in essence, -
Arbitrarily named
Depending on frame of reference.
Within magic angles formulas strangle themselves,
And as far as you can look
You're locked in children's books on a shelf.
The rhythm becomes boring
The reader is snoring his indifference,
But the lyric must flow
So on with the show as evidence.

Private Eye

It was a dark and stormy night,
It seemed the rain would never end.
I was beneath a motel light,
With just a bottle as my friend.

And then the door burst open wide,
And through the fog rolled her perfume,
And then the woman stepped inside,
And spent the night inside my room.

Don't ask me why,
I'm a private eye
Who's still adding up the clues.
I dig the mines
In between the lines
That you're reading in the news.

She was a woman with no past,
I was a man without a plan,
And we made love that didn't last,
Beneath a Casablanca fan.

I awoke to an empty bed,
Then it was clear what she had done,
She'd left a lump atop my head,
And took the bullets from my gun.

Don't ask me why,
I'm a private eye

Who's still adding up the clues,
I dig the mines
In between the lines
That you're reading in the news.

It seems there was a nasty tale
About a mansion on a hill,
And a young widow in a veil,
Who stood to profit from the will.

But then I thought about the rain,
About a tip that she let slip,
A word that led me to a train,
Where now she's handcuffed at my hip.

Don't ask me why,
I'm a private eye
Who's still adding up the clues,
I dig the mines
In between the lines
That you're reading in the news.

The Sea Witch

The mate in the crow's nest blinded by sun,
Saw the horizon rolled in a disguise,
While off to the stern the whole crew did run,
The captain took the helm without surprise.

The waves would pound like a broken church bell,
When the hollowness of the night unfurls,
In a vacuum between heaven and hell,
The sailors were combed away by the curls.

Visions of sea serpents grew within cliffs,
Visions of devil whales' fire crests,
The captain remained to sink with his ship,
Fixing his eyes on the distant clouds' breasts.

Damn it all you fools,
Unclench your fist!
It is she that rules
All nights like this.
You fear burning pools
And frying mists,
But her flames are cool,
They'll meet the sea witch.

Dreams of Plymouth's old colony astray,
In Essex grew a sickness of fears,
The nightmare of Salem would have its day,
Before the golden days of privateers.

The sea is a mirror of the earth's life,
Gray faced it watched a fisherman drown,
And the comfort for his black veiled wife,
Was her hanging for the death of the town.

Well no tombstone could hold her linen soul,
Oceans take to give the fishermen life,
And he must admit the voyage was cold,
He will be warmed by his wife.

Damn it all you fools,
Unclench your fist!
It is she that rules
All nights like this.
You fear burning pools
And frying mists,
But her flames are cool,
They'll kiss the sea witch.

The Tune Suffering

I saw him last night,
Young guy on the street,
It was only by happenstance,
That we should meet.

He thought I was strange,
Saw my double take,
He didn't know the reason why
My heart would break.

Of many roads, there is a choice,
Of many words, there is a voice,
Of many loves, there is a heart,
Life is a play, so learn your part.
Wish I knew then, what I know now,
But you can't change it anyhow,
There's nothing like, the song you sing,
When you learn the tune suffering.

Didn't hear a word
Thought I was insane,
As I said watch out for the storm,
On came the rain.

How was he to know?
How was he to see?
It was so many years ago
And he was me.

Of many roads, there is a choice,
Of many words, there is a voice,
Of many loves, there is a heart,
Life is a play, so learn your part.
Wish I knew then, what I know now,
But you can't change it anyhow,
There's nothing like, the song you sing,
When you learn the tune suffering.

View from an Expressway Overpass

Capsules speed below me,
In an instant they become,
Ghost riders of the past,
And couriers of time.

Woman of the ID

She was stopping all the traffic,
She was piling up the cars,
When you woke up on the canvas,
Looking up at all the stars,
And you heard the birdies chirping,
Circling all around your head,
Saying she's not just a knockout,
She's the woman of the id.

Some hope to find perfection,
Most end up with something less,
You thought you'd find a sex symbol,
Who somehow you would impress,
And I don't know how you did it,
But congratulations kid,
She's not just a classic beauty,
She's the woman of the id.

But promises are broken,
Just as fast as they are spoken,
Certain things you can't avoid,
You could even ask Sigmund Freud.
But she's the one you wanted,
And she stole the heart you flaunted,
Never had the time to skid
Into the woman of the id.

You can call her as a witness,
You can put her on the stand,

You can place her at the murder,
Smoking gun still in her hand,
She'll say she can't remember,
Or understand what she did,
You'll get no explanation
From the woman of the id.

In the summer of our passion,
We might sign away our lives.
Better hope your love is honest,
'Cause no other kind survives.
If she changes like the weather,
You can push down on the lid,
But you can't contain the pressure
Of the woman of the id.

Some eyes are known to travel,
Just as tapestries unravel,
If you lose a masterpiece,
Who can you call, the love police?
And she'll go on undaunted,
While by the question you're haunted,
Is she real outside your head?
Or just the woman of the id.

The Spirit...

Believe

Do you see the bigger picture?
Look at it down below.
Believe and you'll find the answer
In what a child would know.

Do you see the tiny fragment
That bonds to form the whole?
Believe and you'll touch the raiment
That illuminates the soul.

Believe there is something greater,
Believe something above,
Believe and sooner or later,
You'll touch the hand of love.

Why is it that people suffer?
Why is there so much pain?
Believe that the road is tougher,
When there is more to gain.

Once it seemed a vine was growing
Into a wall and died,
But there was a rose still blooming,
Just on the other side.

Believe there is something greater,
Believe something above,
Believe and sooner or later,
You'll touch the hand of love.

Each day is a day of testing,
Each day a smile and tear,
But only in final resting,
Will paradise appear.

Believe there is something greater,
Believe something above,
Believe and sooner or later,
You'll touch the hand of love.

Bet You Always Knew

You should have known my father,
Well now, there was a man,
He left long strides to follow...
I do the best I can.

And if you knew my mother,
You would be pleased to find,
When they say the word "lady,"
It's her they have in mind.

I married a great woman,
Just like my father did,
And we learned about loving
The day we had a kid.

People that I worked for,
I fired them at last,
Selfishness and bitterness
Are masters of past.

And people ask "what's the secret?"
But they won't break the rule.
You see they don't want to hear it,
Not if it isn't cool.
But it's really God and country,
And it's a love that's true,
It's a home and a family...
I bet you always knew.

Now arrogance and hubris,
They like to share a smirk,
I pass them every day,
Along my way to work.

I dig deeper and deeper
To find integrity,
The bottom of barrel
Reveals the best in me.

And people ask "what's the secret?"
But they won't break the rule.
You see they don't want to hear it,
Not if it isn't cool.
But it's really God and country,
And it's a love that's true,
It's a home and a family...
I bet you always knew.

A Better Place

Labyrinthine was the path I took
Through the forest to the river bank,
And whether I will sink or sail,
Now I only have myself to thank.

Unbeknownst to me, I built a boat,
Every day, as I worked and I played,
I'll know which time was better spent,
When by the river it will be weighed.

I see you waving from the shoreline,
With tears on my face.
Just believe we'll meet again one day,
In a better place.

I can see a figure beckoning,
With the power to command the tide,
And he can see what's inside me,
Even through the misty other side.

Now the thief has come and left again,
Taking what was never mine to keep,
My eyes at last have opened up
Here on the day when I fell asleep.

I see you waving from the shoreline,
With tears on my face.
Just believe we'll meet again one day,
In a better place.

Butterfly

Mourn not my end,
Feel joy, my friend,
For once was I,
A butterfly

Emerald Green

The sun will be warm today,
And golden to light his way,
The sky at its truest blue,
So much like the friend I knew.

It's strange to see him up there,
Just yesterday he was here,
But what is a man to say?
The boy has a game to play.

Up on an emerald green,
Up on a higher plane,
The fairway is so serene,
That's where he will remain.

I think of when we played ball,
The laughter that I recall,
Us sharing a Christmas meal,
And the feelings that are real.

It's part of the life we knew,
I'm holding it all for you,
A gift for the moment when
You and I will meet again...

Up on an emerald green,
Up on a higher plane,
The fairway is so serene,
That's where he will remain.

How you used to practice so,
But in case you didn't know,
Although golfers may come and go,
You will always be a pro...

Up on an emerald green,
Up on a higher plane,
The fairway is so serene,
That's where he will remain.

The Light

Walk within yourself,
Past the shadows of today,
Through the silhouettes
Of every failure you have ever known,
Until you come upon a light,
Shining more brightly
Than a thousand suns.
This light shines,
Not from the stars of your potential,
Or from the many things people tell you to be.
There is a brilliance
That has been within you all along,
A light burning with the wonder
Of all the things you already are

Today's The Day

So many times, I took the wrong path,
I was a victim of my own choice,
Then all at once I found the right road,
Today's the day I heard His voice.

So many times, I did the wrong thing,
I didn't know that something was planned,
Then all at once I saw the reason,
Today's the day I took His hand.

Today's the day I felt someone walking
Right there with me, side by side,
And now a flame will burn on forever,
Light my spirit, deep inside.

So many times, I didn't listen,
Or turned a deaf ear to what I'd heard,
Then all at once there were the trumpets,
Today's the day I heard the Word.

So many times, I tried to ponder,
Why do we suffer in so much strife?
It's all because away we wander
From the truth, the way and the life.

Today's the day I felt Him walking
There with me side by side,
And now a flame will burn forever,
Light my spirit, deep inside.

And then I ask what of tomorrow?
What if I falter? What if I fail?
But I can bear with any sorrow,
Today's the day beyond the veil.

Today's the day I felt Him walking there
With me side by side,
And now a flame will burn forever,
Light my spirit, deep inside.

The Soul…

Checkmate

The old man was a master,
But that's not what you would guess.
In life he was a loser,
But he'd never lost at chess.

The boy was in a corner,
Although only in his teens,
And so, he played the devil
For a prize beyond his means.

There always is an option.
And it never is too late,
There's always a solution,
Even if he says: "checkmate!"

The park looked like a prison
To the old man through the fence,
He watched them play for hours,
Filled with tension and suspense.

He thought of his own choices
And the way that he'd behaved
His future had been squandered,
But this boy could still be saved.

There always is an option.
And it never is too late,
There's always a solution,
Even if he says: "checkmate!"

The devil said you're beaten
And the boy started to quit
And to hand his soul over,
When the old man had a fit.

He pointed to the pieces,
There was one move left to win,
He gave the boy his wisdom,
Because silence is a sin.

There always is an option.
And it never is too late,
There's always a solution,
Even if he says: "checkmate!"

The devil took his pitch fork,
Slithered back into the dark,
Faded into the shadows
And then vanished from the park,

But on the wind his whisper
Said: "we'll meet on another day."
The old man said: "be ready
And listen to the words I say...

There always is an option.
And it never is too late,
There's always a solution,
Even if he says: "checkmate."

The Joke

The gates are now closing,
With their iron goodbyes,
The black cars are leaving
With the rain on their eyes.

Try finding a punch line...
But there's nothing to say,
When racing against time,
It always ends this way.

It's like a game you can dominate,
But you never seem to win,
And it's the irony of our fate
To hear the joke at the end.

It was eerie the day
I saw that face again.
It seemed to laugh, to say,
"I am waiting my friend."

It's so simple, I thought,
"We're only straight men,"
He who lives for applause,
The last laugh is on him.

It's like a game you can dominate,
But you never seem to win,
And it's the irony of our fate
To hear the joke at the end.

And do you remember?
He always loved a joke,
A double entendre
In every line he spoke.

The caretaker's raking
Through the long rows of stones.
Are spirits awaking?
Or are we all alone?

Yes, death can be seen here,
With its mute jigsaw face,
It doesn't remain here,
It lives in the lives we waste.

It's like a game you can dominate,
But you never seem to win,
And it's the irony of our fate
To hear the joke at the end.

History…

Bill of Rights

They lived through tyranny,
By royal decree
And saw another way
Beyond the sea.
These are the principles
They built to stand
Throughout the centuries,
Laws of the land:

That any citizen
Was free to speak
And give the government
His own critique.

That a militia
Could bear their arms
And not be people that
A despot harms.

That anyone's own home is
Their castle keep
And not a barracks where
The soldiers sleep.

That we will be free from
The dreaded night
Of a search or seizure
Without the right.

They lived through tyranny,
By royal decree
And saw another way
Beyond the sea.
These are the principles
They built to stand
Throughout the centuries,
Laws of the land.

You cannot accuse me
Of any crime
Without the due process
All in good time.

And those who can judge me
Will be my peers,
And if I am guilty,
I'll pass the years

In retribution for
What I've done,
You will make my prison
A humane one.

And those who may govern
Will never gain
The powers people
Will all retain.

They lived through tyranny,
By royal decree
And saw another way
Beyond the sea.

These are the principles
They built to stand
Throughout the centuries,
Laws of the land.

They gave to a nation
A balanced line
Between the manmade
And the divine.

And they placed the power
Where it should be,
Among the people,
Forever free.

They lived through tyranny,
By royal decree
And saw another way
Beyond the sea.
These are the principles
They built to stand
Throughout the centuries,
Laws of the land.

Society…

Another Angel Flies

Now the morning's turned to black,
You can't hear an ember crack,
But for the good of the neighborhood,
They can bring a building back.

A tear from a widow lands
On the flag held in her hands,
And looking cute with his sad salute,
Beside her, the toddler stands.

And each time their duty calls
Another siren cries,
And each time a hero falls,
Another angel flies.

It's a strange way to behave,
To the people that they save,
Just stand in awe, here we are before
All the bravest of the brave.

After all the smoke and flame,
Just a picture and a name,
The "bestest" dad gave all that he had
Now we'll never be the same.

And each time their duty calls
Another siren cries,
And each time a hero falls,

Another angel flies.

From the Bronx across to Queens,
We should all know what it means,
The banner's hung and the hymns are sung
Where an empty shoulder leans.

At the end of the parade,
When the bagpipe notes all fade,
We should be kind to those left behind,
For the sacrifice they made.

And each time their duty calls
Another siren cries,
And each time a hero falls,
Another angel flies.
And each time they leave their homes
Another alarm wails,
And each time a hero falls,
Another spirit sails.

And each time their duty calls
Another siren cries,
And each time a hero falls,
Another angel flies.

Australia

I watch the flowers wither,
While those in power dither,
Seducing to come hither,
While the pathway is really yon.

I hear the voices quaver,
And promises that waver,
Then along comes the paver,
Behind him history is gone.

So, we can't move to Australia,
We've got to hang tough,
We're not Hamlet and Ophelia,
Enough is enough.

Was kind of them to mention
The lord at the convention,
But there is no exemption
The day that judgment comes upon…

All of those who've done something,
And others who've done nothing,
Who didn't learn that one thing,
Before the day they travelled on.

So, we can't move to Australia,
We've got to hang tough,
We're not Hamlet and Ophelia,
Enough is enough.

Reporters are like parrots,
Dipping their beaks in clarets,
And tightening their garrets,
As we just let them have their fun.

The bloom is off the roses,
But everyone supposes,
Just before the door closes,
They'll make it out as the last one.

So, we can't move to Australia,
We've got to hang tough,
We're not Hamlet and Ophelia,
Enough is enough.

The desperation's mounting,
It's time for an accounting,
And they'll be no dismounting,
Not until liberty is won.

Forsaken is the founding,
But freedom's still resounding,
And its bells will be sounding,
Before it is all said and done.

So, we can't move to Australia,
We've got to hang tough,
We're not hamlet and Ophelia,
Enough is enough.

Balderdash

So, again your explanation
Begins with the word "so,"
Before your pontification
About what you don't know,

As you act as the appraiser
Of what your neighbor's worth,
Looking at outdated photos
You found on Google Earth.

Balderdash, you're full of balderdash,
Balderdash, you're always talking trash.
Well hello Sherlock, now here's a clue,
I've got a secret,
You never knew,
You're full of balderdash,
But I'm through talking to you.

Then you speak of economics,
That you learned from a sage,
But do those late show comics?
Ever tell you "act your age?"

While we're left here with more people
Who've become unemployed,
You'll just splash another puddle,
Once this one's been enjoyed.

Balderdash, you're full of balderdash,

Balderdash, you're always talking trash.
Well hello Sherlock, now here's a clue,
I've got a secret.
You never knew,
You're full of balderdash,
But I'm through talking to you

So, you've got your confirmation,
'Cause you read it online,
Unintended consequences
Are never your design.

Still some bones are in your closet,
Some junk is in your trunk,
Tell us how we should be living,
'Though you're no Buddhist monk.

Balderdash, you're full of balderdash,
Balderdash, you're always talking trash.
Well hello Sherlock, now here's a clue,
I've got a secret,
You never knew,
You're full of balderdash, but I'm through talking to you.

Being in a PowerPoint,
Is not proof that it's real,
And webinars and Skype
Don't mean you touch and feel.

And just having a smart phone,
It doesn't make you smart,
And showing us a plumber's crack,
It doesn't mean it's art.

Balderdash, you're full of balderdash,
Balderdash, you're always talking trash.
Well hello Sherlock, now here's a clue,
I've got a secret,
You never knew,
You're full of balderdash,
But I'm through talking to you.

Balderdash, you're full of balderdash,
Balderdash, you're always
Talking trash.
If you don't like it,
Then don't be crass,
Tweet me at hash tag kiss my...
You're full of balderdash,
But I'm through talking to you.

Desalegn

His name was Desalegn,
He was a soldier of peace,
It's a part of his life
That he could never release

And back in Africa
He had the world at his feet,
But in America
He was a bum in the street.

He wore a uniform,
Ribbons and medals aglow,
He was an officer,
That was many years ago.

Once a leader of men,
Even a scholar at math,
Until defeat in war
Led to a different path.

Desalegn, Desalegn,
I may never know the rest of your story,
But somehow in the end,
I hope to see you in all of your glory.

"They'd kill me back there now,"
He said, reduced to a smile,
But new dangers arise
When you're a foreign exile

There was a factory,
Where he was underemployed,
Then the downsizing came,
And it opened up a void.

And it's a barren land
For a man without a skill,
The stairs you travel down,
Are just a slow way to kill.

Desalegn, Desalegn,
I may never know the rest of your story,
But somehow in the end,
I hope to see you in all of your glory.

The women he once had,
Soon wouldn't recognize him,
The light that lit his eyes
Was beginning to grow dim.

Desalegn, Desalegn,
I may never know the rest of your story,
But somehow in the end,
I hope to see you in all of your glory.

The soup kitchen fed him,
But still he started to drink,
Then the muggers showed him
Just how far down they could sink.

Detested, evicted,
And then a ward of the state,
Arrested, convicted,

He was sick and losing weight.

His name was Desalegn,
He was a soldier of peace,
It's a part of his life
That he could never release.

And back in Africa,
He had the world at his feet,
But in America,
He was a bum on the street

Desalegn, Desalegn,
I may never know the rest of your story,
But somehow in the end,
I hope to see you in all of your glory.

Indian Summer

Now that the smiles have circled my tepee,
And the blue coats have all but moved on,
When the white man can no longer see me,
These souvenirs are all he wants.

And yes, I can see the summer weather,
Thank the Great Spirit for this late sun,
But I'll hold no false hope in October,
As the summer dies in my arms.

So, take the rest of what remains,
For I can see the end of my time
Reflected in the drooping eyes,
Of the last buffalo upon the plains.

Just let me mount inside my mind,
And dream the same dream one last time,
Just let me mount inside my mind...

Invincible

Once upon a fairytale,
In a magic age,
We were like the characters,
Living on the page.

Driving in convertibles
Through the summer nights,
Speed was just an afterthought
As we beat the lights.

But how great to be invincible,
The innocence of youth,
That we're still here is a miracle,
And we're the living proof.

Living in a wonderland,
One just never sees,
Where the road is taking them,
Forest for the trees.

Then you ride a phantom train
Past the auto wrecks,
All the broken promises
A junkyard collects.

But how great to be invincible,
The innocence of youth,
That we're still here is a miracle,
And we're the living proof.

Life is such a precious thing,
Ah, but who knew then?
Used to live so carelessly,
But I won't again.

You could find your destiny,
Just around the bend,
Let yourself discovery it,
And don't let it end.

But how great to be invincible,
Once you can see the truth,
That each day's another miracle,
And we're the living proof.

Roberto

"Papa don't fly tonight,"
The premonition of a child,
It was just another flight,
And to the danger he just smiled.

Mountains will fall to sand,
And take everything in their wake,
If only a plane could land,
It was a chance he had to take.

Oh, I have seen fields of heroes
Taking noble stances in the hall,
And the image of Roberto
Is there among them upon the wall,
But if you stop there don't forget
How he answered when he heard the call,
And the legend of Roberto
Is in a place that will never fall.

Always he'd be the one
To bring it all home on his own,
And his work was never done,
As long as one child was alone.

Wreckage lies on the sea,
So far below a darkened sky,
Up there he has to be,
Because he'd wouldn't pass them by.

Oh, I have seen fields of heroes
Taking noble stances in the hall,
And the image of Roberto
Is there among them upon the wall,
But if you stop there don't forget
How he answered when he heard the call,
And the legend of Roberto
Is in a place that will never fall.

Shadow of the Cheetah

The elephant's the master,
The lion is the king,
But I'm the one who's faster
Than any living thing.

I'm crossing the savannah,
And just about to pounce,
Chasing an impala,
And tracking every bounce.

I'm pursuing, he's evading,
We're both doing what we must,
Yet the wilderness is fading,
Like his hoof beats in the dust.

Now the herds they have been thinning,
And it's hard to catch the scent,
Still the shadow of the cheetah
Will be the last to relent.

I blend in with the grasses,
My coat is my disguise,
Until at last it passes,
The moment of surprise.

The reason he was living
Was to become my kill,
But I need no forgiving,
I only take my fill.

See the burning sun surrender
To the stars that light the night,
Like a glowing sketch they render
All the legends of our might.

Now the herds they have been thinning,
And it's hard to catch the scent,
Still the shadow of the cheetah
Will be the last to relent.

Sights of a Rifle

We color the clouds like the sprinkles on ice cream,
Just spinning on spoons licked by the wind
That silently carries us down out of a dream.
The barrels shine, like a soul that's not sinned.

From heights in the distance the land is serene,
But there flickers a flame in the dark,
'Though the face of the forest is painted in green,
Falling deeper our sights see a spark.

And on my fear fed a feeling
That something was wrong
As the boy held me whispering
An old barracks song.

It seems we are falling faster now into the sound
Of thrashing, cracking, scraping, tearing,
The toll that must be paid before we reach the ground,
The treetops punish us for our daring.

And although we can't see the tiger in the night,
Still somehow, we can feel him staring,
And then in a flash of light, so begins the fight,
With so many of us just hanging.

And on my fear fed a feeling
That something was wrong
As the boy held me whispering
An old barracks song.

Then machetes flashed,
To the marsh we splashed
With the battle plan dying...
And my sights were set,
And my ears went deaf,
But still I remember the crying...

And on my fear fed a feeling
That something was wrong
As the boy held me whispering
An old barracks song.

Now the port of Haiphong has been mined at its mouth,
The muddy monsoon covers my eyes,
The bombs fall to the north, but we're moving south.
They load me with slugs they call supplies.

Then the pressure on my trigger is released,
The hand on it quivers, as it bleeds,
Down the medics come to take him up the rungs,
And the chopper leaves me in the weeds,

And on my fear fed a feeling
That something was wrong
As the boy held me whispering
An old barracks song.

Still destined to shoot,
I was kicked by a boot
And I heard Charlie's laughter
Now he's found a friend.
So, I'll fight again,
Am I a slave or master...

Spirit in the Air

Watch closely, or you'll miss it,
Just like a shooting star,
From childhood to tomorrow,
The journey isn't far.

He walked into the darkness,
A storm that raged inside,
Wanting to be who he was,
And all their love and pride.

And it happened in an instant,
Just moment of despair,
And where once there was a guard rail,
Suddenly, nothing's there.
So today the Hudson River,
Is just flowing like a tear,
And swallowing the promise
Of a spirit in the air.

And as we light our candles,
And as we say our prayers,
We have to hold the spirit,
Before it disappears.

For always an accomplice,
Will take us to the edge,
So, someone has to help us
To walk across the bridge.

And it happened in an instant,
Just moment of despair,
And where once there was a guard rail,
Suddenly, nothing's there.
So today the Hudson River,
Is just flowing like a tear,
And swallowing the promise
Of a spirit in the air.

Tales of the Forgotten Sea

The pirate ship cut its way
On through the yellow sun,
Came aboard the tiny boat,
And soon their work was done.

And deft to the young girl's scream,
They threw her to the deck,
Blind to their dagger's gleam,
They held it to her neck.

But still the boat people
Set their sails and die just to be free,
And who will ever know
All the tales of the forgotten sea.

The young boy could not just stand
And watch their evil touch,
Even for his tender age,
He loved the girl so much.

He fought hard, but soon would shrink
Into a pool of red,
And once again hopes would sink,
And pirates would be fed.

But still the boat people
Set their sails and die just to be free,
And who will ever know
All the tales of the forgotten sea.

Tiny Soldiers

Tiny soldiers march on their way,
It's do or die on the field today,
For reasons they don't understand,
And consequences that no one's planned.

Got to win if you want to play,
Remember kid, what the grown-ups say,
"If you want to be a man, my boy,
Don't treat that cowhide ball like a toy."

March tiny soldiers, march,
Freeze your tears.
March tiny soldiers, march,
Hide your fears.
Rusted armor
Will show the damage done,
A shell-shocked man
Was once a wounded son.

Stand tall there in your uniform,
Don't complain about an aching arm,
Forget talk of girls and sissy love,
You'll catch all your treasure in your glove.

The losers hang their heads in shame,
While the winners learn to hate the game,
Dad makes the majors in his son,
While squandering a fortune of fun.

March tiny soldiers, march,
Freeze your tears.
March tiny soldiers, march,
Hide your fears.
Rusted armor
Will show the damage done,
A shell-shocked man
Was once a wounded son.

The ringing echoes of the war,
Still haunt them like a creaking door,
So, they return to prove their skill,
But echoes linger, always will.

Cold steel trophies mark what's missed,
And one day their own kids will enlist,
Remember that they grow up fast,
Sometimes with a crippling past.

March tiny soldiers, march,
Freeze your tears.
March tiny soldiers, march,
Hide your fears.
Rusted armor
Will show the damage done,
A shell-shocked man
Was once a wounded son.

Tragic Flaw

From high atop some precipice,
Far beyond the warning signs,
Some curious eyes may wander
Across the very same lines,

That can trace your footsteps fighting
Through the hard luck of the street,
To the office of the sentry,
And to where you and he meet,

And so, practiced is his handshake,
It hides a retracted claw,
And you won't even feel it,
'Til he finds your tragic flaw.

What face will the future give to
This scenario and its sleuth?
Will machines he deemed qualified,
To judge the applicant's truth?

And what will mark their existence?
The procedures of their chore?
They are bound to fade with changes,
Like a waterline on a shore.

Who will see the interviewers?
Perhaps moth balls in a draw,
Where they'll lie like worn out garments,
That now bear a tragic flaw.

So now, open now your closet,
Let your skeleton come out.
Don't be ashamed to be naked,
With many others about.

Countless spirits have confessed here,
And then passed on through the wall,
Left their secrets in this prison
Where he tripped them up to fall.

And whether or not employed here,
They could find the exit door,
But the sentry remains behind,
That remains his tragic flaw.

About the Author

Edward Kenny has written over a thousand song lyrics and eight musicals. He first entered the Broadway scene in 1982, when *Valhalla*, a musical he co-wrote with his longtime collaborator, composer/arranger Val Angrosini, received a first-class option. Material from the show was aired on television in conjunction with the *Hempkompst* expedition, a recreated Viking dragon ship which sailed from New York Harbor to Oslo, Norway. "*Valhalla*" was previewed by *Broadway Tomorrow Musical Theatre*, and was selected as a finalist in the New York drama league grants competition. The New York foundation for the arts awarded a grant to present "*Valhalla*" as a performance art work.

The World Goes On, a song from *Valhalla*, was aired on WGBB 1240, where Val and Ed were interviewed. At that time, two songs that they had written to commemorate the tragic events of September 11, 2001 were played, along with other original material.

Two additional musicals by this writing team, *Goodnight St. Petersburg* and *Straight to the Ace*, were also previewed by *Broadway Tomorrow Musical Theatre*. Material from the shows was also aired on the New York City cable television talk/variety show *What's Going On*, where Val and Ed appeared as guests.

Straight to the Ace was nominated for the *Dramatists Guild* musical theatre program. It was also nominated by the *American Academy of Arts and Letters* for the *Harold Prince Musical Theatre* program. *Purple Cow Playhouse, Ltd.* presented the show under a grant from the New York State Council on the Arts. *Ace* was also presented in *New York City* by Craig Slivka at the *Chelsea Playhouse, The Producer's Club*, "*The John Houseman Studio Theatre*

II, Theatre 22, The Home Theatre, and the *Frederick Lowe Room of the Dramatists Guild.*

The Angrosini/Kenny collaboration began in 1979. The two have penned hundreds of songs which have been performed by Val's original bands at *The Right Track Inn, Paulson's, Catch a Rising Star, The Brokerage,* and other metropolitan area clubs. Their theme song for the group *Amethyst* was aired on television commercials.

Ed was a finalist in the Babylon citizens' council on the arts (BACCA) annual songwriting competition. His original songs have been aired on WUSB and WGBB radio, and on the television series *PM Magazine.* He studied poetry and lyric writing while attaining his Bachelor's Degree at Adelphi University.